Cornish Ra

St Austell to Penzance

CRAIG MUNDAY

KEY
Books

BRITAIN'S RAILWAYS SERIES, VOLUME 6

Title page image: 66006 is seen departing Treviscoe on the Parkandillack branch on 26 February 2014 with the lagoon in the foreground.

Contents page image: 43185 negotiates the reverse curves through Coombe St Stephen with the 09:00 Penzance to Paddington on 24 January 2017.

Cover image: Colas Rail's 60047 pauses at St Austell between showers on 30 January 2016.

Acknowledgements

I would like to give thanks to the following people for their help with the book. Andy Thomas deserves special thanks. He has been my 'wingman', supported me throughout and given me the huge privilege of showcasing some of his excellent pictures for the book. My family has played a huge part over the years, so thanks to the Mundays: Morven (dad), Scott (brother), Clare, Katie and Abby. A great team has helped in checking the content, so thanks to Andy Thomas, Nick Dyke, Martin Duff, Bob George and Emily Maiden. Also appreciated is the support of Trevor Maxted, Roger Geach, Rich Lewis and Martin Street.

I would like to dedicate this book to my friends and colleagues who supported me in the early days: the railwaymen who encouraged me to join the industry and supported my enthusiasm – Les Askew, Dave Pond, Simon Franoux, Ian Blackburn, Steve Rickett, Ken Magor, Jimmy Burt, Mark O'Brien and especially Roger Matthews; and the band of friends who followed the railways and were an endless supply of enthusiasm and companionship, especially in the early days – Steve Clemo, Andy Richards, Gis Harris, Andy Sheppard and George Richards.

Published by Key Books
An imprint of Key Publishing Ltd
PO Box 100
Stamford
Lincs PE19 1XQ

www.keypublishing.com

The right of Craig Munday to be identified as the author of this book has been asserted in accordance with the Copyright, Designs and Patents Act 1988 Sections 77 and 78.

Copyright © Craig Munday, 2020

ISBN 978 1 913295 98 1

Typeset by SJmagic DESIGN SERVICES, India.

Contents

Introduction

Welcome to my second volume about the railways of Cornwall. This book focusses on the railway lines from St Austell to Penzance and the existing branches still running. In addition to this, the Hayle Wharves branch has been included, the only line in the volume that no longer exists. The branch was close to my home in Hayle, and was the start of my fascination with railway operations, so I felt it worthy of study.

The areas covered in this volume are very close to my heart, as I grew up in Hayle, and currently live in St Austell. I consider the railway west of Burngullow especially beautiful, so any opportunity to grab a picture of a loco hauled train in the Coombe St Stephen area, or Probus is always capitalised upon.

The early 80s produced some remarkable scenes on Cornwall's railway – the last of the Class 25s, and the final workings to Hayle Wharves, St Erth milk sidings and Holmans at Camborne. My composition skills were minimal in those days, but I was so glad to have obtained some Hayle Wharves shots which have been reproduced in magazines. In 1986, I obtained an Olympus Trip camera and this brought much better results. The ever-changing railway saw garish new liveries appearing such as Network Southeast and the raspberry-ripple InterCity colours. Railfreight grey locomotives gradually replaced the all-over blue we were so used to.

Then in 1989 I joined British Rail as a signalman in East Cornwall. Based at St Germans, I was a reliefman covering St Germans, Liskeard and on occasions Largin. This brought me up close to the industry I had always loved. A while later, I applied for signalling vacancies in West Cornwall. I was stationed initially at Roskear Junction and then as a relief signalman, which allowed me to cover all the signal boxes between Truro and Penzance. My eyesight not being up to scratch for driving, this was the next best thing. The traction was varied, and plentiful. I worked my way up to become a controller at Swindon and Cardiff from 1994 to 2006, so there is a gap in my West Country photography and I'm grateful to Andy Thomas for filling this. I dabbled with video cameras from the late 90s to the present day, which led to a downturn in still images. I obtained a compact digital camera on my return to Cornwall as a mobile operations manager in 2007. This was fine for bright sunny days, but no use for trains moving at speed.

By the mid noughties, the traction and workings were becoming rather predictable. Class 66s had swept aside all the freight class locos we treasured. Class 37s became rare. We also lost the last loco-hauled regular workings, the TPO, parcel traffic and CrossCountry services. These transferred over to Voyagers with the odd HST thrown in. First Great Western HSTs dominated the InterCity workings and DMUs the local ones. The line west of Burngullow has been especially affected by this. The withdrawal of the weekly fuel train in 2013 left the GWR Night Riviera as the only booked loco-hauled service in the area running all year around. The summer Saturday loco-hauled GWR service from Penzance to Exeter and return was a popular photographic study in the years it ran, giving a hint at the once plentiful supply of loco-hauled departures from Penzance in previous decades.

The dawn of SLR cameras being available to all saw a change in many photographers' habits. My other photo interest is Cornwall and its landscapes, particularly the coast. With photo opportunities now pre-planned, I took more interest in the landscapes surrounding the railway. Angles of the sun could be studied, and the passage of the trains could be followed online, a far cry from the 1980s when you simply stood on a platform and snapped away.

Telephoto lenses allowed a perch 0.5 miles from the track, or indeed, on the opposite side of a riverbank to take shots. This has channelled my photography to this day. Many books about the railway in Cornwall have been produced over the years, and I wanted a slightly different approach from these.

The seasons have always fascinated me. The changing landscape, long days of high summer and short days with piercing low sunlight all have an appeal. My favourite time of year is undoubtedly the golden eight weeks as I call them; the four weeks either side of 21 June (the longest day). This allows maximum daylight, and importantly the sun rises and sets with the optimum angle. The upside of the Cornwall main line is that it is lit this time of year, allowing a different perspective. Websites such as Suncalc (www.suncalc.org) accurately indicate where the angle of the sun will be throughout the year, and the difference in the arc of the sun's travel between June and December is stark. As with the previous volume, all the seasons are shown and a variety of traction featured. This is not a 100 percent three-quarter angle range study as I believe this has been explored many times before.

Beginning at St Austell, with the clay workings as a backdrop, the industrial scenery gives way to rich arable farm land on the way to the capital city. West of Truro, the landscape is littered with former mine workings and signs of its rich industrial heritage. West of Camborne the line passes the busy fruit farms and proceeds on to my childhood home town of Hayle. Once across Hayle's unique viaduct, the line passes through St Erth before passing St Michael's Mount, skirting Mounts Bay, and finishing at the terminus of Penzance.

The branch lines are also featured, including the only freight-only branch still running from Burngullow to Parkandillack, along with the passenger branch lines of Truro to Falmouth and St Erth to St Ives. As mentioned, the Hayle Wharves line has a special focus.

Chapter 1

St Austell to Redruth

Departing St Austell, the line crosses two wonderful viaducts, St Austell (also known as Trenance) and Gover, and the waste tips from the china clay workings dominate the skyline. Burngullow, a rather forlorn sight these days, is next. Only the East London-bound sand traffic loads here, and other freight services merely pass time or combine at this former busy clay installation. The freight-only line to Treviscoe and Parkandillack diverges here. With the exception of the night sleeper, loco-hauled services have become very scarce west of Burngullow in recent years. Onward, the line travels into rich arable land towards Crugwallins and Coombe, then on to Trenowth and Grampound Road. Probus is next, and since the single line was re-doubled in 2004, the casual observer would never realise that this section of line had ever been singled. The line then runs through dense vegetation and through two tunnels, Polperro and Buckshead, prior to reaching the county's capital city, Truro. Truro retains its signal box and semaphores, and heading west it shares a bi-directional line with the busy Falmouth service through Highertown Tunnel. The main line then curves to the right at Penwithers Junction and heads into farmland once again as it travels towards Tomperrow (Threemilestone) and Baldhu. The ever-expanding city of Truro is now noticeable across the skyline with new building projects inevitably binding once separate villages together. The line sweeps onward through Chacewater and then climbs to meet the A30 trunk road at Hallenbeagle, where the first remnants of the copper industry come into view. A fine example is the former engine house at Scorrier which is still standing proudly beside the line. The town of Redruth begins to unfold at the site of the former Drump Lane yard. The short Redruth Tunnel heralds arrival at the railway station.

The cutting approaching St Austell is quite photogenic, despite not being able to accommodate a long train. On 23 March 2019, Class 50s 50007 (renumbered 50014) and 50049, in GBRf livery, worked from London Paddington to Penzance and returned to Waterloo. This marked 25 years since the final BR-operated Class 50 railtour, *The Terminator*, which was also promoted by Pathfinder. The weather was particularly grim that day.

To the west of St Austell, the main line crosses two masonry viaducts, the first one being St Austell Viaduct. The afternoon Treviscoe to Carne Point clay is seen heading east hauled by 66055 in the attractive bright red DBC livery on 2 October 2019.

The second viaduct is Gover Viaduct. On a bright evening on 4 June 2013, one of the GWR power cars, 43186 (adorned with advertising vinyls for HP 'all change'), powers west with 1C86, the 15:03 Paddington to Penzance. This is a high-summer shot, with the sun extending around to illuminate the upside of the line, showing the green trees in high definition. St Austell Viaduct is visible in the background.

This image is taken from the concrete overbridge visible in the previous image. It shows the 11:00 Burngullow to Exeter Riverside presenting a very corporate image, with matching locos and wagons, on 25 February 2019. The train was running double headed with 66035 and 66149 due to engineering work in Devon.

Burngullow is the next railway location on the journey. Once a thriving English China Clay railway hub, loading a variety of powdered and slurry china clay products, it was the commencement point for the 'silver bullets' bogie tank trains to Irvine in Scotland. This traffic is no longer supplied from Cornwall. St Blazey depot proudly maintained the Class 37/5s, which worked this service in pairs throughout. On 27 February 1990, a Class 56 was trialled in Cornwall to see if the class would be a contender to replace pairs of Class 37s on the longer distance services. 56013 was the loco involved and is pictured at Burngullow. It worked on a variety of clay workings around mid-Cornwall, and famously visited Penzance to assist an ailing Class 47, 47815, on the down sleeper service, which had failed near Par.

On 15 December 1986, 47191 draws down the branch from Parkandillack with a long rake of loaded clay hood vacuum braked wagons. The former Burngullow Junction signal box, closed in October 1986, can be seen beyond the bridge. It was kept for some years after closure as a mess-room for maintenance staff but was burnt down in 1996.

On 16 August 2016, 43091, in blue livery, leads a GWR green set past Burngullow, working the 11.00 from Penzance to Paddington. The line curving away to the right above the leading power car is the freight-only branch line to Parkandillack.

The monopoly of red- or maroon-liveried DBC Class 66s was broken in 2019 when one of the Maritime-liveried members of the class was diagrammed on the Burngullow sand circuit. 66162 stands at Burngullow on 29 August, with the first portion of loaded wagons, waiting for its path eastbound after the 1A83. The loco returned from Exeter light loco later in the afternoon, and then worked the second portion from Burngullow just after 20:00 that evening. The wider shot has been included to illustrate the rather barren looking former loading area, with just a road-railer stabled for overnight work that week.

To the west of Burngullow, the clay industry still dominates the skyline. The massive clay tip at Nanpean has become covered in grass in recent years. The engineering trains in the Duchy see a fair variety of freight operating companies (FOCs). On 14 November 2014, Freightliner Class 66/5s 66548 and 66547 work a long train of Falcon wagons west past Crugwallins.

With menacing clouds sweeping in from the Newquay direction, a pair of Class 150/2 units in slightly different GWR blue liveries hurry towards Burngullow at Crugwallins with 2P86, the Penzance to Plymouth service, on the same day as the previous picture.

50004 *St Vincent* drifts downgrade from Burngullow, past Crugwallins, on the late summer afternoon of 25 September 1987, with the 11:45 Paddington–Penzance. The Blackpool clay dries stand out in the distance. The rationalisation work to single this section of line from Burngullow to Probus is clearly evident with the alignment of the old down line still visible. Fortunately, the line was re-doubled in November 2004. (Photo © Andy Thomas)

On 30 September 2006, Kingfisher Railtours ran a trip from Clapham Junction to Penzance with EWS-liveried 37406 *The Saltire Society* as the traction. The weather in Cornwall that day was unkind with bands of heavy rainstorms frequently passing through. A particularly nasty one can be seen in the background over St Austell, but just down the line at Dowgas, near Coombe, the sun made a fleeting appearance just at the right time. (Photo © Andy Thomas)

The reverse curves near Coombe are a splendid viewpoint for eastbound trains in the morning. Long trains can stretch right back giving a superb switchback look to the train. On 2 August 2018, GWR Class 57 57603 is seen hauling a failed HST set back to Laira as 5Z77. The leading power car is 43027 in the 90 Glorious Years commemorative livery.

On the same evening, bang on time some 15 minutes after the previous picture was taken, 57605 works 2C51, the 17:50 Exeter St Davids to Penzance, across Coombe Viaduct. This was where I loved to capture the west-bound loco-hauled train, with blue loco and matching stock. Due to the setting sun, it had to be between May and July (the golden eight weeks). The sun would catch the train perfectly, provided it was on time. It was scheduled to leave St Austell at 20:09, following a series of down GWR and CrossCountry services. On many occasions a bright forecast was scuppered by a thin veil of cloud or mist to the west, which saw the light drop significantly, or all together, as the hum of the Class 57 could be heard approaching.

The following year, the reliveried green Mk3 day coaches were starting to appear in the consist. The blue stood out much better against the greenery at Coombe. A bonus on 4 July 2015 was DRS hired in 57303 making an appearance on the service. This image is taken deeper in the fields and even in early July, the setting sun is making an impact on the trees below the viaduct.

The morning view of Coombe Viaduct from the high fields on the down side of the line is becoming obscured by massive trees growing up from the valley below. Mrs Round's fields are now in the background as WCR's Class 47/7 47746 heads back to Plymouth with former LMS steam loco 6201 and its support coach on 18 September 2018.

Heading down from Coombe, Fal Viaduct is next. More secluded than Coombe, nearby fields give a fine view of a down train mid-morning. 2019 saw the final year for slam door HST sets in traffic, so this would be the last autumn for such trains passing. 43160 leads a mix-match set west with a stopping service on Sunday 25 August 2019.

Two views from the attractive village of Trenowth, near Grampound Road. More sweeping curves add to the picture as the morning low winter sun does its best to burn off the mist hanging in the area as Colas Class 70 70807 powers a rail delivery train back from west Cornwall on 16 December 2016. The bare trees and barren landscape contrast with the bright livery on the locomotive. The village of Grampound Road can be seen in the background.

The same location on 23rd May 2015. The lineside vegetation is now alive with rhododendron as DRS Class 57 57303 works the GWR loco-hauled stock up to Par to start 2P70, the 11:25 to Exeter St Davids. During the initial years of the train running, it ran empty from Long Rock to Par, while in later years the service picked up passengers from St Erth.

Unlike their General Electric Class 70 counterparts, the designers did a superb job of styling the Class 68 locomotives, incorporating a sports car look, giving them a rakish front end and an attractive livery. With the added benefit of a far more vocal-sounding power unit, they have instantly become popular with enthusiasts. Cornwall has seen a number of the DRS locos visit, mainly on railtour duties, but they have also made appearances on NMT workings too. With the fields already harvested by 30 July, 68017 hurries west with empty stock from a charter in 2016. This image was taken from the fields overlooking Trenowth, near Grampound Road.

Another view of the reverse curves at Trenowth, this time from the upside in high summer. The HST's final summer in charge of the long-distance Paddington services saw 43030 lead 1C86, the 15:03 Paddington to Penzance, west towards Grampound Road on 19 July 2018.

The sweeping curve at Resparveth is probably one of the finest photographic locations in Cornwall as it is blessed with no lineside vegetation and a fine vista back towards Crugwallins in the background (the turbine is visible top right). The royal DBC Class 67s 67005 and 67006 were allocated onto the Belmond Pullman trips on Saturday 23 April 2016, and it ran in fine light. The train drops down from Grampound Road, bound for Truro. A Class 66 was added on the rear to assist with shunting at Truro.

A slightly wider summer shot sees the view in full bloom as the Saturday afternoon CrossCountry 1V48 York to Penzance HST purrs downgrade at Resparveth on 30 July 2016. The power cars were 43357 and 43321. Until recently, this was the only opportunity to see a CrossCountry HST west of Plymouth. Cows have replaced sheep in the field nearest the train.

From Grampound, Probus is next. Both had stations until the 1960s but little remains at Probus these days, except a few stop signals. The shadows are growing and sunlight is diminishing as 2C51, the Exeter St Davids to Penzance, passes the former station and heads for Truro on 16 July 2016, hauled by 57603, which had a mixture of Mk3 coach liveries in tow. The village and church stand out in this view.

Illustrating how overgrown the railway line towards Truro from Probus is, on 22 August 2016 a green-liveried Class 150/2 and blue Class 153 combination work a Penzance to Plymouth service across Tregarne Viaduct.

Two tunnels herald the approach on the down to Truro. Polperro is the first, and this high-summer shot taken from the cutting shows 43151, leading the 1C86 from Paddington, about to enter the tunnel on 16 June 2015.

The railway between the tunnels is deeply overgrown, and there is no realistic opportunity for any photography. This image, taken at the Truro end of Buckshead Tunnel, was shot during vegetation clearance in the area prior to an inspection of the tunnel portal. Looking like a model railway, two Class 150 units, 150123 and 150266, head for Truro with 2C48, the 15:55 Plymouth to Penzance. This service was widely known as the Primark express, as Cornwall at the time had no store, and many shoppers would return from Plymouth with the trademark brown paper bags in tow.

An access point near the new homes and over bridge at Kenwyn near Truro gives a fine view of down trains approaching the viaducts. On 22 April 2017, 43017 leads a Paddington to Penzance service out from Buckshead Tunnel. The brick base remains and decayed wood are all that's left of a former plate layers' hut at the location.

Two fine viaducts, high above the city below, usher down trains into Truro. Truro Viaduct is followed by Carvedras Viaduct. The Crown Court, opened in 1988, stands between the structures and can be seen at the bottom left of the picture. The RHTT visits Falmouth on Sundays, and the return working is seen heading back to Par on 7 October 2018. This was the first visit during that season and was worked top and tail by 66120 and 66200.

The view from the signal box in the early 1990s was very different from that of today. The cathedral was visible and there was little of the lineside equipment that can be seen today. I was grateful to my colleague, Phil Hancock, at Par for the tip-off that 47803 was working 1Z50, the Derby to Penzance, on 3 May 1993. This replaced the 06:48 HST from Dundee that day. It was a unique infrastructure-liveried Class 47/8 but was often drafted in to work in the passenger fleet when required. The rear of the train is still crossing Carvedras Viaduct.

Class 46s disappeared from the network in 1984, and in 1986 Class 45s were banned west of Bristol. This resulted in me having few good images of them working in Cornwall. 1C11, the 06:50 Swindon to Penzance, and the 13:52 return to Bristol Temple Meads were a favourite for the class, as was the 18:10 Penzance to Bristol in the mid-1980s. Class 45/0 45022 *Lytham St Annes* waits time at Truro on 1F84, the 18:10 from Penzance, one evening in August 1984. It has received some embellishments with white window and grille surrounds and buffers, and a red buffer beam. St Blazey driver, Ken Mitchell, leans from the window as the parcels and mail are loaded. This was a leisurely trip up from Penzance, with lots of parcels being loaded. The BRUTE trolleys containing the post for the Royal Mail train (19:22 from Penzance) can be seen on the other platform ramp.

The up main departure shot from the box window is now hampered by railings and other railway furniture. In September 1986, 50019 *Ramilies* stopped ahead of the starting signal with a long train. The driver was Plymouth man, Roy 'Boxcar' Wilce. A lovely chap, well known for the bootlace ties he used to wear. The crossing barriers were much wider apart in those days and also protected the through lines behind the signal box.

The 12:15 Penzance to Paddington parcels train used to recess in the down platform at Truro to allow the 12:40 from Penzance to overtake. It was a favourite service for the trainee Plymouth drivers to work with their traction inspector, as it had a propelling move. The long van train used to pull past the signal box and then set back into the platform, using the east end crossover. 47543 is seen departing Truro after the manoeuvre in March 1993. This lay-over would be unthinkable nowadays, due to the busy 30-minute timetable. Note how the level-crossing barrier has been relocated to beside the up main line. In previous years, the barriers also protected the eastbound lines behind the signal box and spanned a large area, rather like Red Cow crossing at Exeter St Davids. Passengers alighting at Truro station and walking down the platform ramp were now much more protected then in the image above!

The remodelling of the level crossing at Truro is also illustrated here with Colas Class 70 70806 heading back to Westbury, after delivering a Railvac to the yard on 28 Jun 2016. Judging by the A2B coach at the crossing barriers, there was probably some railway disruption that day. The town houses on the right of the picture stand where Truro down sidings, and latterly Vospers car dealers, once stood.

50013 *Agincourt* and 50037 *Illustrious* cause some excitement for a young lad as they draw into Truro with the lengthy 12:10 Penzance–Glasgow parcels on 26 August 1983. The long train and loaded BRUTE trolleys on the platform illustrate just how much of an integral part of the railway the movement of mail and parcels once was. 50013 was one of the Class 50s refurbished at Doncaster without receiving the large logo livery at the same time – the headlight is an obvious giveaway. (Photo © Andy Thomas)

6 September 1985 was an eagerly awaited day for many. The first run of a steam locomotive on the Cornish mainline since the 1960s took place from Truro using GWR Castle class locomotive 7029 *Clun Castle*. Two photos are included showing the crowds filling the station and over bridge at the west end of the station. The locomotive stands at the west end of the station at Truro.

Also on 6 September 1985, 1C11, the 06:50 Swindon to Penzance, was worked by Class 45/0 number 45003 and is seen departing Truro with many heads peering out of the train windows at the steam locomotive on the right of their train.

Truro was heavily rationalised in November 1971, when the station was reduced to the now familiar two through platforms and down side branch bay. The signal boxes at Penwithers Junction, Truro West and Truro East were consolidated into Truro East, and simply renamed Truro Box. Until January 1988, it was possible to access the up yard from either end of Truro, but the junction was removed, resulting in two long sidings and a shorter one accessed from the west end only, beneath the over bridge. 37175 is seen shortly after arrival from St Blazey in August 1986 with a single air-braked VDA wagon. 37175 was briefly allocated to the south-west and was modified with CP5 self-steering bogies. The permanent way department had concerns about the damage Class 37s were doing to the infrastructure.

50016 is seen stabled in the through sidings behind Truro station, in May 1985. The office block to the left was the Area Manager, Mr Rusty Eplett's, office. The loco and stock from the previous day's 15:27 Penzance to Plymouth had failed and limped into the yard. 50016 was the rescue locomotive.

The present-day Truro yard sees many of the lines replaced by car parking, and palisade fencing protecting the area. Network Rail has a sizeable maintenance depot here too. Colas Class 70 70806 is seen delivering a Railvac machine stabled in Truro yard on 28 June 2016.

Heading out of Truro we pass through Highertown Tunnel, and then Penwithers Junction. GWR Class 57 57603 is seen running into Truro on the up main and is about to enter the short tunnel on 2 July 2016, working the Saturday only Long Rock to Par empty stock service.

The line west from Penwithers Junction passes through farmland and dense lineside vegetation, making photography difficult. The lineside opens up east of Chacewater near Penstraze, giving a splendid view of Tallicks bridleway crossing in the background. The Sunday morning Belmond Pullman empty stock to Truro traverses the reverse curves with matching liveried DBC Class 67s 67021 and 67024 on 29 April 2018. The spring blackthorn blossom and gorse are out, adding to the sparkling light that morning.

The former station at Chacewater is the scene for the Penzance to Paddington with 47816 in charge, taken on 3 August 1994. The down platform is still in evidence, but the up platform was removed long ago.

One of my favourite images of 2016 is the Cornish banksides covered with flowering rhododendron. Sadly, the flowers do not last long, but they are a beautiful spectacle. The embankment west of Chacewater is breathtaking, with 43023 passing, working 1A89, the 13:00 Penzance to Paddington, on 31 May 2016.

Climbing out of Chacewater, the land supporting the former triangular junction to Newquay via Perranporth has been obliterated by the A30 trunk road near Scorrier. On 14 September 1993, Class 117 DMU set 117305 in chocolate and cream livery passes under the bridge by Smoky Joe's cafe.

The view towards the Redruth direction, taken with heavy telephoto, enhances the reverse curve past the former Wheal Busy siding signal box. The former mine working at Hallenbeagle, Scorrier, and colourful gorse complement the 1A81 on 20 April 2017.

Weekend track relaying in the Treleigh area of Redruth saw the down line removed on 14 January 2014. Colas Class 70 70807 sits on the up line with a train of Falcon wagons.

The former Drump Lane signal box closed in January 1986. The former down refuge sidings were to the right of the locomotive, and a new housing development has sprung up where Harris's bacon factory once stood. Class 47/8 47816 works a westbound Paddington to Penzance on 18 August 1990.

The final years of Class 47 haulage on FGW had its fair share of problems and reliability issues, and substitutions were relatively common with other companies' Class 47s being hired on a regular basis to supplement the small, but hard-worked, home fleet. On 14 September 2001, one of the regular substitute locomotives, Fragonset-owned 47709, is seen here accelerating away from its Redruth stop and passing the remains of Drump Lane yard with 1A45, the 08:20 Penzance–Paddington. (Photo © Andy Thomas)

The railway from Drump Lane into Redruth runs through a very built-up, and run-down industrial backdrop. The sun does make an appearance mid-morning in the deep cutting. An interCity-liveried power car makes a rousing start from Redruth station and leaves the short tunnel bound for Truro in May 1987. The Paxman Valenta engines in the power cars were rather smoky, as illustrated here.

50009 *Conqueror* pauses at Redruth station in January 1987, with snow still evident on the platform. Penzance driver, Joe Hall, waits for the tip to take the afternoon stopping service westbound. (Photo © Scott Munday)

Looking westbound from the platform, the Carn, with its imposing castle and monument, overlooks the station. A RES Class 47/4 passes with the 12:10 Penzance parcels train in May 1993.

Chapter 2

Redruth to Penzance

Redruth station's buildings have been tastefully restored and recently painted. Over Redruth Viaduct and into the shadow of the Carn and its monument, the area is scarred with the rich mineral extraction of years gone by. The former station at Carn Brea is passed, and then come a series of level crossings controlled by the updated Roskear Junction signal box. The junction and crossover are now long removed at Roskear so there is now a straight run into Camborne station. Dropping once again, through Penponds and by the fruit and vegetable (sadly no longer carried by rail) fields around Gwinear Road, the line crosses Angarrack and Guildford viaducts. The sand dunes of the Hayle Riviere Towans can be spied in the distance. In less than a mile, the train enters the small town of Hayle, my home town for the first 21 years of my life and responsible for the railway coursing through my veins! The station is now a mere halt; no signal box remains and there is only a footpath to identify the former goods branch line to the wharves that so fascinated me as a child. Next, the line runs over the unique Hayle Viaduct, the region's former engineering heritage still visible below for now, but the area is fast being developed. Onward, the line goes across the causeway and runs beside the estuary teeming with bird life, then heads away from the north coast into St Erth station. The station has been renovated and now has modern features. The branch platform has been widened to accommodate the increased recent patronage. This is due to St Erth replacing Lelant Saltings as the St Ives line's park and ride station. The final steep bank and semaphores are encountered departing St Erth and the line heads to the south coast once more, where St Michael's Mount looms into view. Skirting the coast along Mount's Bay, and along a single track passing the extensive GWR depot at Long Rock, the journey's end is Penzance.

The railway runs almost level between Redruth and Camborne, and the industrial area around Carn Brea is not the most scenic in Cornwall. However, atop the Carn there is a wonderful view. The north coast and St Agnes can be seen in the distance in this 21 October 2016 view of the once-a-month Friday run of the NMT HST passing below.

The HST fleet that have worked the Western Region long-distance express trains have carried many liveries since their introduction in 1976. Inevitably, some have been smarter and more eye catching than others. A First Group-liveried set passes through the industrial landscaped at Carn Brea with the 09:15 Paddington to Penzance on 21 March 2004. The picture is enhanced by the large amount of gorse along the railway in this section. (Photo © Andy Thomas)

Just west of Carn Brea is Brea village; the railway runs above it on an embankment. In this 4 June 2016 view, the Saturday loco-hauled empty stock catches some nice sunlight as it enters the cutting, having just run along the embankment. The loco is 57603 and is in spotless condition here, a credit to GWR.

The embankment at Brea is the scene for the returning fuel tanks from Long Rock in 2013, the final year the depot saw fuel delivered by rail. 66066 works the empty tanks back to St Blazey on 15 February.

On 21 September 2017, Colas Rail's 66849 works a crew training trip to Penzance. It passes Brea, heading for Dolcoath crossing. To the far left, the winding gear of South Crofty mine is visible. Hopes remain for a resurgence in mining in the area, and South Crofty would be the most likely contender to resume production.

In August 1991, 47804 is seen powering away from Camborne station in the cutting just east of Roskear Junction signal box. The train is an InterCity-liveried loco with Network Southeast stock, which would normally have worked commuter services out of Paddington to Newbury and Oxford on weekdays. On weekends, they worked far and wide in the early 1990s. The service is the 12:35 Sunday only Penzance to Paddington.

In the final summer of HSTs on the Paddington run, I photographed many of the London-bound services passing the box. 43185, in the InterCity Swallow livery, was a favourite. It worked 1A87, the 10:46 Penzance to Paddington, on Monday 22 April 2019. The Camborne area is dissected by three level crossings. The newly commissioned Dolcoath obstacle detection (OD) crossing replaces an early 1960s automatic half barrier crossing (AHBC). The next crossing is Roskear barriers at Stray Park Road, and the third crossing is at the London end of Camborne station. The signal box, in which I have spent many hours, controls all the crossings in the area, and is beside the down line here.

Just as the HSTs faded from main-line services in 2019, Class 50s did the same in the early nineties. On 30 August 1990, 50037 *Illustrious* passes the box on a lovely summer's evening with an Exeter to Penzance relief train. This was one of the final service trains on which I photographed a Class 50. The former route branch to Roskear, and latterly Holmans siding, can be traced to the left of the brick platelayers' hut beside the fourth coach in the formation. This line closed in the early 1980s, although the track remained for some time afterwards.

The railway west of Burngullow hasn't seen much freight since the 1980s and 37670, working a short ballast train, was worth photographing in September 1991. The loco expired just after this picture was taken, and a Class 47 from Penance came to rescue it.

Taken from the footbridge adjacent to the signal box, 37207 unusually works the 18:10 service from Penzance in the spring of 1987. I caught this picture by complete chance. 37207's days were numbered in Cornwall as the *William Cookworthy* nameplates had been removed by the time this picture was taken.

The section of up line between Camborne and Truro, 14 miles in length, was governed by just one signal until the resignalling scheme of October 2018. R4 signal stands on the platform at Camborne, and generations of enthusiasts have watched trains waiting for their signal here. 50026 *Indomitable* pauses at Camborne in August 1986 with 3S15, the 12:00 Penzance to Glasgow parcels, which was given about 10 minutes dwell time here.

Moving west from Camborne, the line drops away to Gwinear Road and crosses Penponds Viaduct. The viaduct is all but hidden by trees, but the line levels out past the fruit and vegetable fields. On 26 April 2016, WCR Class 57 57316 heads west with the Statesman tour. The Carn is visible in the background.

The event of Mazey Day, or the Golowan Festival, at Penzance is an important date for loco photographers. For many years, railtours have visited the resort on that day. In previous years, as many as three separate excursions have dropped off festival goers and rail enthusiasts in equal numbers to the town. In recent years, Spitfire Tours no longer trades, and Pathfinder are the only operator to run. Mazey Day falls on the third Saturday of June, and for years this coincided with the GWR loco-hauled service too. On 23 June 2018, Class 50s 50049 and 50007 worked the Pathfinder tour down and made a splendid sight with their matching blue carriages. Knowing it was a long rake of coaches left us with a dilemma as to where to capture the whole train in a picture. The Class 50s and all 13 carriages are in this Gwinear Road view.

On a fine summer day, 47624 brings the lunchtime parcels 1A90 Penzance to Paddington towards Gwinear Road in June 1994. Evidence of the old station platforms is still visible some 30 years after closure. The train is about to cross the AHB crossing at the Camborne end of the former station.

The design of a Class 55 Deltic is impressive and thankfully many railtours have brought both 55009 and 55022 to Penzance; the first recorded visit was in September 1997. The locos have visited in both green and blue liveries, and Mazey Day 2012 saw 55022 *Royal Scots Grey* work the Pathfinder tour down from Tame Bridge Parkway wearing its 1980 blue livery. The loco was slipping badly because of the heavy train and very wet rails, and speed was down to a walking pace as it roared under Nanpusker Bridge. It took about 30 minutes to reach Camborne, some three miles away.

The field next to Nanpusker Bridge on the Gwinear side is a well-known favourite spot for train photographers. On 28 February 2018, I drove from Par to find Angarrack, near Hayle, like a winter wonderland. I had to park and walk half a mile through deep snow up to Nanpusker Bridge to grab a shot of 150246 working the 2C46.

This classic down line shot at Angarrack captures the daffodils in full bloom. The NMT, running on a sunny Friday morning, couldn't be missed. Power cars 43013 and 43062 drift over the viaduct on 11 March 2016.

43002 *Sir Kenneth Grange* leads 1A83, the 10:00 Penzance to Paddington, over Angarrack Viaduct on the fine morning of 23 June 2018 (also Mazey Day of that year). The village of Angarrack, which is famous for its Christmas light display, nestles under the massive stone structure. Hayle Towans are behind the viaduct, whilst in the far distance, St Ives is visible in the summer haze. (Photo © Andy Thomas)

The view of Angarrack Viaduct from a farm at Gwinear is beautiful. It shows the Atlantic Ocean and sand dunes of Gwithian Towans, along with the trees decorating the valley floor. This viaduct, its yellow-coloured granite piers reflecting the light beautifully, is my favourite in the county. The morning Paddington to Penzance Night Riviera crosses the viaduct with DRS Class 57/3 57303 leading all blue carriages on 15 April 2015. The blue FGW livery stood out so well at these locations, and the new GWR dark green can often appear lost in the landscape.

Once across the viaducts, the railway runs downhill into Hayle station past Ventonleague and Bodriggy. On Saturday 4 June 2016, GWR Class 57 number 57603 powers up the bank from Hayle at Ventonleague with a mixed rake of Mk3 carriages. Penzance driver Lee Mcdonald can be seen driving.

Former LMS locomotive 46100 *Royal Scot* was a very welcome visitor to Penzance on 27 April 2016. The children of Bodriggy School at Hayle were allowed out in the playground to see the steam loco working the *Great Britain IX* railtour. The loco makes a fine sight powering up the bank from Hayle station, and it was a bonus to hear the excitement of the school children as the train approached and passed by.

In the 1980s, Mk3 loco-hauled coaches were a rarity in Cornwall. The afternoon 1M82 14:58 Penzance to Milton Keynes service saw a WCML set diagrammed to the far west on summer Saturdays. It was a heavy train, with up to ten carriages in tow, and sometimes included a Driving Van Trailer (DVT) on the rear. Toton's 47444 *University of Nottingham* climbs the bank from Hayle station in September 1989 and passes Bodriggy school.

The selection of trains taken at my home town of Hayle commences with 47125 derailed just east of the station on catchpoints in April 1982. 47125 was travelling to St Erth, down direction on the up main line. The catch points had not been secured for the movement, and the train tipped over towards the embankment. Luckily, no one was hurt, but it was some time before 46037 arrived with the crane over night to right the loco and rerail the wagons.

On the same day as the 47125 derailment, Class 47/0 47076 *City of Truro* propels the break-down vans through the platform at Hayle toward the stricken train, about 400 yards up the line. Hayle signal box, which can be seen behind the locomotive, was closed by the time the photo was taken and demolished in 1983.

On the gorgeous morning of 30 June 2001, 47831 *Bolton Wanderer* is at the business end of the 08:46 Penzance to Manchester Piccadilly, which is passing through Hayle. The clouds were rapidly gathering in the background over the coast and the sun soon faded. The signal box has been removed from the upside platform and a holiday let in the shape of a former Mk1 carriage resides behind the down platform. (Photo © Andy Thomas)

Class 50 50033 *Glorious* on a glorious day in 1986! The afternoon stopping service from Plymouth calls at Hayle with its trademark Mk1 coaches in tow.

50017 *Royal Oak* was refurbished at Doncaster without receiving the large logo livery straight away. Fellow locomotives 50001, 50006, 50013, 50019 and 50047 underwent the same refurbishment. The loco is seen in 1983, running into Hayle on the up main with a stopping service to Plymouth. Hayle station in the 1980s was a super place to spend a sunny summer Saturday. There were many loco-hauled services to watch, with a variety of traction. It was interesting to see families from other parts of the UK heading home after their holiday, and there was often time to chat before their train home.

My dad usually took cine of the hydraulic locos at work, but thankfully took slides from time to time. From 1968, Warships often ran double headed on the Penzance to Paddington services, giving the driver an impressive 4,400 horsepower at his disposal. In July 1969, D870 and D869, both in maroon livery, work the 11:25 Penzance to Paddington into Hayle station. (Photo © Morven Munday)

There are few remnants of the original Hayle station furniture these days. The empty brackets that carried the red fire buckets still remain though, quietly rusting away. The palm trees also thrive, despite receiving little care. The trees provide a super frame for 57602 working the St Erth to Exeter St Davids Saturday loco-hauled service on 17 June 2017. Lelant station on the St Ives branch is visible in the distance on the right-hand side of the image.

50033 powers away from Hayle in 1986 and passes above the same road twice as the B3301 (the former A30) passes under two spans of the viaduct.

Hayle Viaduct has played an integral part in my railway life for many years. My dad's barber shop was in Foundry Square and he watched trains from the window from 1964 until retirement in early 2006. In the mid-seventies we knew the withdrawal of the remaining hydraulics was imminent and I recall seeing the peaked windows of the Western locomotives awaiting departure from the station on the down line from that window, and the majestic sight and sound of the loco powering away. We watched the diesel electrics take over, and their virtual demise too. Now in 2020, more trains than ever before cross the viaduct each hour, albeit GWR four-car HST sets, multiple units and the Hitachi IET trains. One of dad's slides shows a blue Western locomotive, with a mixture of maroon and blue and grey stock, heading eastbound over the viaduct in 1971. The traffic below was much quieter then than it is today, despite there being no Hayle bypass back then. (Photo © Morven Munday)

The fields near Penpol primary school are often used by the Richards family for growing daffodils. They are a stunning feature in the foreground as the down Night Riviera departs, particularly on a Monday when the service arrives later into the Duchy. With St Ives as a backdrop, 57310 departs Hayle on 10 March 2016. In this study, the dark green GWR livery on the coaches actually enhances the train against the background. Below the third carriage in the train, the buffet car, my father's barber shop, mentioned in the caption above, can be seen. It is the small house-like building with the white transit van outside.

The evening run of a GSMR test train, running top and tail with DRS Class 37s 37038 and 37608, fitted perfectly on Hayle Viaduct on 14 May 2012. I regret very much not discovering this shot earlier, and have taken many images here on Penpol Terrace since.

50011 *Centurion* departs Hayle and catches some late summer evening light on 8 September 1986. 50011 was the first of the Class 50s to be withdrawn the year after this photo was taken and was cut up in Crewe Works.

The Hayle Estuary is teeming with bird life and is one of the hot spots for bird watching in the UK. The trains pass by on either side of it with the main line on one side, and the St Ives branch line on the other. The Hunslet-Barclay weedkiller train was allocated Class 20 traction in the 1980s, with its own drivers conducted by local men with route knowledge. Class 20 locos were extremely rare in the Duchy, just a few pairs had previously visited on the Pathfinder *Chopper Topper* railtours that ran in 1986. The April 1990 trip, worked by 20901 and 20904, is seen on Hayle causeway heading for St Erth.

The final day of Virgin-operated locomotive-hauled CrossCountry services was on 19 August 2002. 47847 and 47840 were specially prepared for the final 08:46 Penzance–Manchester Piccadilly with 47840 *North Star* even reverting to its original number of 47077 for the day. The weather in the Duchy was sparkling for the event and the immaculate pair are seen near the beginning of their historic journey about to pass under the A30 between St Erth and Hayle. (Photo © Andy Thomas)

Her Majesty The Queen and the Duke of Edinburgh visited St Ives on 17 May 2017. The Royal train was worked by Class 67s 67006 and 67026. A Class 66 66201 (in less than Royal train condition) led the train through Cornwall on the down line, due to a GSMR fault on the Class 67s. The departing impressive nine-coach empty stock is seen leaving St Erth, taken from the down refuge sidings, whilst the Queen travelled in style to St Ives aboard a service train worked by 150265.

The down morning stopper sweeps past St Erth box in 1986, hauled by Class 50 50042 *Triumph*. The loco has a secure future in the Duchy, preserved on the Bodmin and Wenford Railway, and sees extensive use through most seasons.

I happened to be in Plymouth on the evening of Saturday 27 July 1985 when a York to Penzance relief train was announced. I saw two St Blazey drivers walk to the end of platform four. A Class 37/0 rolled in and I jumped aboard for a trip to St Erth. St Blazey drivers were the only crews to drive Class 37s in Cornwall. This appearance of a split-box Class 37 in the county was rare enough, but for it to work a passenger train was extraordinary. I later learned that 37058 also worked the same train through, also in July. 37024 is pictured at St Erth in poor weather for a July evening.

The advent of the InterCity livery was very attractive when it was applied across loco and coaches. A Class 47/8 47813 rolls to a halt at St Erth in March 1992 with an inter-regional CrossCountry service. It is likely the locomotive worked the train from Birmingham New Street.

I must admit to not including many images of the new Hitachi IET Class 802s in the book. I have included this evening shot taken from the doorway of the St Erth box because of to the dramatic sky and sun setting behind the station. The Paddington-bound train departs on 20 October 2019. To the right of the picture, the new deeper profile of the bay platform can be seen, as well as the shortened bay siding.

The Western Region's pride and joy, 47835 *Windsor Castle*, passes Rosevidney Bridge, just west of St Erth, having dropped the Queen off in Penzance on 4 May 1990. During that era, Class 47/8s were the dedicated and preferred traction for the Royal train.

The failure of a HST at Truro on 31 May 2014 caused great disruption in the Duchy. Class 57/6 number 57602 was commandeered from its usual loco-hauled passenger duties, 2E75, the 11:25 Par to Exeter St Davids, to rescue the stricken set. The cavalcade passes Rospeath near Crowlas on a beautiful late afternoon. The signal on the left is St Erth's up distant signal and is green for the CrossCountry HST to Leeds.

A panoramic view, taken from the hill near Marazion looking back right across Mounts Bay, shows all the main railway landmarks, including Long Rock depot, Ponsandane, Penzance signal box and the station itself. A Class 150/2 looks quite insignificant working a Penzance to Plymouth service past the former station at Marazion on 11 April 2014.

Looking back towards St Erth from the road bridge on a beautiful summer afternoon, an executive-liveried train sweeps around the curve on the final stretch of its journey from the capital in June 1986. The set number (253036 in this case) was still being applied to power cars at this stage, though set mix ups were common.

With just a trace of exhaust, 47816 *Bristol Bath Road* has the power on having just passed over Long Rock crossing at the start of the lengthy journey east with the 11:40 Penzance–London Paddington on 3 August 2002. (Photo © Andy Thomas)

The GWR depot at Long Rock had its first open day on 13 April 2019, and the stabling roads were filled with visiting locomotives. GBRf's 73107 stands in the sunshine just prior to the gates opening.

From the December 2019 timetable change, slam door HSTs were no longer used by GWR for their passenger service. It was a surprise, therefore, to hear of blue power cars 43171 and 43172 *Harry Patch* running together to Long Rock in January 2020. The depot carried out an exam on the two power cars, and they are seen overnight on 30 January, sharing the shed with a Voyager unit that had worked the 1V62 from Glasgow on 29 January. The depot is now home to the fleet of GWR Class 57/6s; this is the first time a main-line locomotive has been based in the Duchy since they were introduced. Even the St Blazey Class 37s were officially based at Plymouth Laira.

I couldn't resist a cameo appearance in the book, so here's an image, taken by my dad, of a Western passing the old Long Rock depot in 1973, with me watching on aged just four years old. The chemical tanks in the background having no doubt visited Hayle Wharves ICI plant at some point. (Photo © Morven Munday)

This book captures many of the railtours that have visited the Duchy. The Class 40s were very popular visitors on these and the run of D200/40122 in November 1985 was memorable, even though the weather was terrible. The Class 40 Preservation Association's 40145 received a main line certificate, allowing it to visit the county on many occasions. It wore BR green livery for its initial visits, then BR blue in 2006, and latterly large logo livery. The large logo livery was not associated with the class in BR service, but certainly looked colourful on the locomotive! On 26 August 2006, 40145 visited Long Rock for fuel after working a railtour down from Ealing Broadway. The area directly behind the loco has accommodated two 100-ton fuel tankers for many years. These were used to store fuel for trawlers working in the area. The siding next to the Class 40, Old Bank, has been restored to service and is now regularly used to stable GWR trains that have visited the sheds at Long Rock.

The humble Class 08s have been decimated in numbers over the years. GWR still have a handful in use, and two reside at Long Rock, though at the time of writing, 08410 had been sold to a private buyer in Middlesbrough. During the depot refurbishment work, the spare carriages from Long Rock were stabled near the station in Slopers loop, to maximise the space around the shed overnight. 08410 ambles down towards the loop on 10 May 2017.

The *Great Britain* rail excursions have been regulars in Cornwall. These trips often run over four or five days, rather like a land cruise by train. Today, the train is a specially painted rake of vehicles, and has been steam and diesel hauled in recent years. In 1993, Mk1 carriages with white roofs were complemented with a matching liveried Class 47/8 47823. The train is seen approaching its destination at Eastern Green.

50027 *Lion* powers out of Penzance on Sunday 14 August 1983, with the 11:45 Penzance–Liverpool Lime Street. Despite a variety of different coaches in the rake, the uniform livery of the whole train and locomotive made for a smart corporate sight. In just a few years, this corporate image would be lost as a whole host of new liveries were introduced, resulting in mixed rakes of carriages. In the background a three-car mechanical unit rests in the sea sidings after a busy summer Saturday spent shuttling between St Erth and St Ives. (Photo © Andy Thomas)

The BR structure gauging train is seen stabled in Penzance Sea Sidings in May 1987 as the 07:40 HST from Paddington runs past it into the terminus.

Pairs of Class 33s have worked many railtours to Penzance. *The Crompton Swansong* brought 33031 and 33033 to the resort on a bright 29 October 1988. The locos are seen propelling the empty stock back into Slopers siding to run around the coaches.

The 13.30 from Penzance to Plymouth and 15.55 return was diagrammed using the Class 47 and day carriages from the overnight sleeper service. Twenty-one years later the practice re-started on summer Saturdays only, using Class 57s. On 3 August 1993, 47812 works the 15.55 from Plymouth into a sunny Penzance. On this day, a parcel van was in the consist and can be seen behind the loco.

A pair of RES Class 47/7s, 47701 and 47705, propel the parcel vans back into Penzance station to work empty up to Plymouth in the summer of 1994. The signal box behind the train has arguably the best views of any in the UK.

The four-platform station and train shed at Penzance is compressed in this telephoto shot from the box window, taken on Sunday 22 April 2012. The traction typifies the modern railway at that time, with a GWR HST, Voyager and Class 150/2 and 153 multiple units present in this morning view.

One of my early and favourite snaps at Penzance features two Class 45/0 locos on subsequent departures at Penzance. 45077 departs platform four with the 11:35 to Plymouth, whilst 45058 waits in platform three with the 12:00 parcels to Glasgow on 18 June 1985. It was unusual for the 11:35 to produce a Class 45.

In addition to the visit of 56013 in 1990, 56064 visited Penzance with the *Grockle Grid* railtour on 8 May 1995. The loco is seen stabled beside the platforms during the afternoon. (Picture © Scott Munday)

A picture from under the train shed at Penzance. 50023 *Howe* awaits the shed turner driver to release it from the blocks on platform three in 1988. The loco is wearing the original Network Southeast livery.

We finish this chapter with a tremendous shot from Andy Thomas. To have two Class 45s side by side in 1983 is one thing, but having 45036 present with split headcode panels still intact is remarkable. This was the last Class 45 in BR service to have the older-style panels. The bull nose yellow ends with marker lights, as fitted to 45101, were the norm once the locos emerged from Derby Works after overhaul. The date was 6 August 1983 and 45101 saw action that day working the 10:50 to Brighton. In the background, amongst the postal trolleys, an MG 1300 is parked up on the platform dock; it probably belonged to one of the local drivers who was at work. In the days before the onset of pay and display car parks at nearly every station, this casual approach to parking was a common practice. (Photo © Andy Thomas)

Chapter 3

Burngullow to Parkandillack

The freight-only mineral branch from Burngullow to Parkandillack still sees two or three trains a week. The single-line section, controlled by a metal train staff, begins at Crugwallins. Crugwallins was a former loading siding. The line then climbs around a large horseshoe curve to head towards Drinnick. The railways runs behind the village of Foxhole, and the landscape quickly becomes an industrial one. The pathways and roads that criss-cross the area are white from the clay extraction in the area. Man-made hills of waste from the clay industry hug the railway on its circuitous route onward.

The line passes over the road at the former Drinnick works, where clay and coal were carried by train. The coal was for a small power station. It then goes onward to Little Treviscoe, over a level crossing where the nearby massive excavations dominate the area. Passing under the Stepaside road bridge, the loading complex at Treviscoe is reached. Treviscoe has multiple loading areas and covered stores called Linhays. Both CDA and JIA wagons are loaded here. Treviscoe has a large lagoon the water of which, under the right lighting conditions, is electric blue in colour and makes a remarkable foreground study for a passing train. The Treviscoe loading points are reached by a series of three ground frames along the single line (or main as it is called, oddly). It is possible to enter the complex at either end, as the line carries on a short distance to the end of the line at Parkandillack. The landscape here is now dominated by the waste incinerator for the county. This was constructed right next to the railway, but is not rail connected. The Imerys clay calcification plant, as it is officially known, is the final loading outpost in Cornwall. The plant still sees CDA wagons loaded from time to time, though visits of the JIA wagons for loading are very rare.

For five consecutive days in March 2007, special trains, featuring a Black 5 steam engine 45407 supported by Class 37s 37406 and 37410, ran onto Devon and Cornwall branches. On day four, 28 March 2007, the Fowey branch was visited in the morning and Parkandillack in the afternoon. 37406 *The Saltire Society* creeps off the Parkandillack branch at Burngullow. (Photo © Andy Thomas)

Setting off from Burngullow, the Parkandillack branch is very overgrown after diverging from the main line and going around to Crugwallins. Crugwallins (Burngullow Rotary) was once a rail-connected clay loading point, and just beyond the former clay sidings is an occupation bridge. The 38 loaded CDAs are brought up the branch in two portions of 19 wagons due to the weight limit. The bridge arch makes a perfect frame for the second portion as it creeps around the bend with 66066 on 6 June 2016.

The line dissects the pretty village of Lanjeth. School Hill has an open crossing, and trains have to stop and sound the warning horn before proceeding across. Trains on the branch after 4pm are a rarity these days, and this returning ballast train was a movement during an engineers' blockade. Having delivered ballast at Treviscoe from the side tipper wagons, the train ran to Burngullow, top and tailed with 66084 and 66004, on 11 April 2020.

The re-run of the *Cornish Centurion* railtour, the *Cornish Centurion 2* ran on 4 May 1991 from Manchester Piccadilly, repeating the ground covered by the original tour which ran in January 1991. Once again, the motive power in the Duchy was 50008 *Thunderer* and 50015 *Valiant*. Problems with 50008 meant that the run to Falmouth was aborted. Earlier in the day, 50015 leads the tour back off the Parkandillack branch and pauses at the ungated crossing at Lanjeth. (Photo © Andy Thomas)

After passing Lanjeth, the line passes under the St Austell to St Stephen A3058 road at High Street. Here, the railway turns north and heads for the village of Foxhole. The nearby embankment offers a good view of the loaded train on its return from Treviscoe. EWS-liveried 66176 drops down towards Lanjeth with the second portion of CDA wagons on 11 August 2014.

Carpalla crossing is near the village of Foxhole and is used by the owner of a smallholding to transfer animals and vehicles to and from his field. The evidence of former clay workings cover the landscape on the branch line, the tip in the far distance is near the wonderfully named Greensplat, near Roche. The JIAs wagons normally run to Treviscoe on a Thursday and return between 11am and midday. They later form a service to Stoke-on-Trent. 66041 passes the crossing with a long rake of wagons dusted, as if with icing sugar, with china clay from the loading process at Treviscoe. The blackthorn blossom adds some extra colour on 16 April 2015.

A lane crosses the line at the Nanpean end of Foxhole and is a good vantage point to photograph the returning loaded train. 66092 passes with a rake of CDAs to combine at Burngullow to make the full train onward from Burngullow to Carne Point on 11 April 2014.

Class 37s 37670 and 37401 are deep in china clay country at Little Treviscoe heading for the end of the line with the *Cornish Parker* railtour on 16 May 2009. (Photo © Andy Thomas)

Another view of Little Treviscoe, looking back to Drinnick as the engineers' train powers away from the worksite markerboards on 11 April 2020. The bright gorse colours and redundant track panels add some interest to the scene.

With the all-important pixie mascot on the lamp bracket, DB Schenker-liveried 66152 provides a splash of colour at Little Treviscoe crossing with the *Cornish Explorer* railtour from Eastleigh on 20 September 2014. 66080 was on the other end of the train. (Photo © Andy Thomas)

The Parkandillack branch has hosted many railtours over the years. On 9 June 2012, 37606, with 37609 on the rear, works the *3-2-C* railtour from Crewe to Parkandillack past the crossing at Little Treviscoe.

Colas-liveried 37116 took a trip up to Parkandillack on 13 May 2020 on a crew training outing. The loco is seen passing Little Treviscoe crossing on the return leg. This image was taken with social distancing measures in place during the COVID-19 pandemic, and Andy Smith can be seen in the second man's seat wearing a facemask, as was driver Alan Peters.

The Imerys clay facility at Treviscoe has a number of rail loading points. Movements here take some time as wagons are loaded and moved along the linhays by the train locomotive. 66027 has pulled its wagons up to the headshunt at Kernick ground frame on 12 April 2016 and is ready to form up its train, which will then run to Burngullow Junction via the track in the foreground.

Class 37 37606 rounds the curve at Kernick clay dries, Treviscoe, with 1Z21, returning from Parkandillack to Crewe via the Heathfield branch, on 9 June 2012. (Photo © Andy Thomas)

Early on the morning of 22 September 2014, DB Schenker-liveried 66152 worked up to Parkandillack with CDAs for loading. The return loaded working ran in two portions; the first as 6P23, the 13:30 Parkandillack–Burngullow, which is seen passing Kernick clay dries at Treviscoe. (Photo © Andy Thomas)

Photography at a clay works is often tricky. The bright sun is ideal for the shot, but the reflection against the clay powder deposited everywhere can cause over-exposure. On 8 June 2015, 66078 waits at the end of the linhay for the CDA wagons to be loaded by dumper truck.

The linhays themselves can provided a novel frame to an image, as seen here at Treviscoe when a rather smart 66020 was positioning JIA wagons for loading on 23 August 2018. The dark sky behind warns of an imminent downpour.

The line continues on from Treviscoe to Parkandillack. This loading facility is not as busy with trains at Treviscoe but still sees CDAs loaded from time to time. Class 66 66078 shunts the wagons in the complex on 8 September 2015. The large building under construction to the right is the Cornwall waste disposal incinerator. It was built right next to the line, though not rail connected.

On 16 May 2009, Class 37 37401 stands at Parkandillack waiting to depart and tackle the steep gradient up to Treviscoe with a railtour that originated from, and was returning to, Crewe. This image shows how rural a location this was until the construction of the adjacent incinerator. (Photo © Andy Thomas)

St Blazey driver Steve Burton looks back at his train on the straight at Parkandillack on 15 September 2014. The train staff covers the section from Crugwallins right up to the buffer stops at Parkandillack. This results in only one train being able to be on the branch at one time. To the rear of the train are the points for the run around loop and beyond that the buffer stops. During the 1980s, there was a proposal to close the current Newquay line and run the passenger service from here across to St Dennis Junction (reinstating around two miles of track).

Chapter 4
Truro to Falmouth

The branch line from Truro to Falmouth, named the Maritime Line, is now one of the busiest stretches of railway in the Duchy. The installation of a passing loop and signalling at Penryn in 2009 has allowed a 30-minute service pattern. The trains are busy throughout the day, and the Penryn campus, part of Exeter University, has led to many students to taking the train.

The branch leaves the mainline at Penwithers Junction, just outside Truro, and unlike many slower branches the speed rises to 50mph shortly afterwards. The line runs through dense woodland areas and through the first of the tunnels, Sparnick Tunnel; both tunnels on the line were built to double-track gauge. The countryside opens out somewhat as the train passes over Carnon Viaduct and then into Perranwell station. The line runs through farmland towards Perran Tunnel, near Ponsanooth. The main road interchange from Helston, Redruth and Penryn is then passed under at Treluswell, and the line descends to Penryn. Here, a Falmouth-bound train runs onto the passing loop, around the waiting Truro-bound service and into the platform. This innovative design allows both trains to utilize the same long platform, the Truro train at one end and the Falmouth-bound one at the other.

Back onto a single track once again, the train runs across the beautifully curved Collegewood Viaduct. To the eagle-eyed on board, the river is visible here across to St Mawes. The suburbs of Falmouth are soon reached, and the line boasts three stations serving the town. Falmouth itself is a large town in comparison to most coastal ones in Cornwall. Penmere, delightfully maintained by the Friends of Penmere station group, is the first station. A short distance on, the most central station for the town centre is next. This was once called the Dell, but has since been named Falmouth Town. The final stretch runs to the terminus of Falmouth Docks. The passing loop and rail connection for freight to the docks was removed some years ago. A single platform, complete with overall roof, is all that remains.

19 July 2017 was a day of sharp showers and sunshine. 150102 heads towards Penwithers Junction with a Falmouth–Truro service. County Hall is starkly lit on the hillside behind.

The Sunday RHTT trips are the only scheduled loco-hauled services on the Falmouth line. 66238 and 66160 work the 4 December 2016 trip along the cutting, recently cleared of vegetation, near Sparnick Tunnel. Despite being only four weeks before Christmas, a lot of autumnal colour is still visible in the tree tops.

In the last moments of sunlight at 20:33 on 15 May 2010, 40145 makes a surreal sight crossing Carnon Viaduct heading for Falmouth with the *East Lancs Champion* railtour, which had arrived at Penzance earlier in the afternoon. (Photo © Andy Thomas)

Perranwell itself is around half a mile from the station. After departing Perranwell station, Falmouth-bound trains pass along an embankment overlooking the village. The half-hourly service means four train movements an hour pass by here, so there is no need to linger long for a photograph! A pair of Class 153s in contrasting blue FGW livery head towards Falmouth on 30 April 2015.

In April 2014, the *Great Britain VII* railtour included as part of its itinerary a visit to, and steam out of, Falmouth. The train had arrived in the county the previous day and had stabled overnight at St Blazey. On the morning of 27 April 2014, the train ran from St Blazey, empty coaching stock, to St Austell to pick up the passengers and then head to Falmouth where double-headed steam would take over for the next stage of the multi-day trip. 47746 was the traction for the diesel-hauled legs and it is seen near Perranwell heading for Falmouth. (Photo © Andy Thomas)

Trewedna Water is a small wooded area between Perranwell and Perran Tunnel. The area was cleared of vegetation in 2017, and photos opportunities not seen for many years were available once again. During this period, two shuttles worked the 30-minute interval Falmouth services, one booked for a pair of Class 153s, the other one a Class 150 diagram. These are scheduled to pass each other at Penryn. 150129 passes Trewedna road bridge on 27 April 2017 with a Truro bound service. Class 150/2 are now the booked traction for both services, though a Class 158 has deputised on rare occasions.

Two Class 153s exit Perran Tunnel and head for Perranwell, the liveries on the units contrasting nicely with the bluebells decorating the tunnel cutting sides on 8 May 2017. 153370 had received the then new GWR green livery, whereas 153333 still carried the Visit Devon promotional vinyls.

On 25 August 2013, the Maritime line commemorated its 150th year of operation. A visit of a HST was arranged, and specially invited guests took a trip along the line. 43005 is the leading power car and the down train is seen passing Penryn. This image shows the passing loop to the left of the train, and the points converge beside the photographer. As can be seen, the platform continues on to provide access to the Falmouth-bound portion of the train.

Despite the date being 2 November – some weeks into the 2014 autumn programme – the locos employed on the west country circuit aren't too dirty. 66090 and 66017 cross Collegewood Viaduct, situated just west of Penryn, and are seen from the Penryn station perspective.

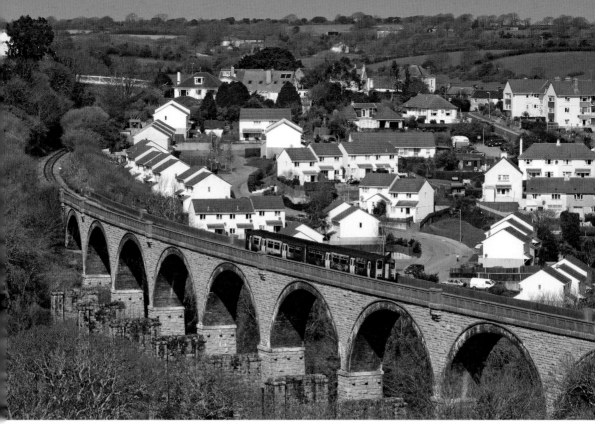

With all the decorative vinyls making the train look like a mobile bill board, a Class 150 crosses Collegewood Viaduct after having stopped at Penryn. It is making one of many journeys from Truro to Falmouth on 24 March 2007. (Photo © Andy Thomas)

The beautiful curved Collegewood Viaduct is seen to best effect from the Penryn side. However, there is no river view here! The RHTT was eagerly awaited when the sun shone. On 18 October 2015, 66061 and 66238, viewed adjacent from the Penryn bypass, head for Falmouth. Photographers are keen to capture the train early in the leaf fall season as the train becomes filthy two or three weeks into the programme.

The Network Rail NMT was scheduled to visit Falmouth on 3 June 2016. The train is seen at Falmouth Docks station with power cars 43013 and 43014. To the right of the train is the track bed for the former lines down to the docks. Some of the recently lifted track from the former run round loop can be seen stacked to the right of the HST.

It's hard to believe that this sylvan setting is actually the approach to one of Cornwall's largest towns, Falmouth. On 15 May 2010, 153377 drifts in on the shuttle from Truro. (Photo © Andy Thomas)

The *Cornish Gnome* railtour on 3 May 1998 originated in Cardiff and brought green-liveried 37403 into the Duchy. At Truro, local St Blazey engine 37669 was added to the rear for the trip to Falmouth. The empty train sits at Falmouth Docks prior to 37669 heading back up the county to Looe. (Photo © Andy Thomas)

A two-car mechanical DMU rattles to itself under the platform awning at Falmouth Docks on 17 February 1983, after arriving with the 14:50 from Truro. At the time ,set P471 was allocated to Laira. (Photo © Andy Thomas)

Chapter 5
Hayle Wharves

The small branch line from Hayle station to Hayle Wharves housed an Esso fuel delivery depot and an ICI works. The ICI works produced Bromine, and the plant closed in 1973. This resulted in only fuel being delivered until the closure of the branch line in 1981. There was a power station at Hayle too, but coal came in by boat from Barry in South Wales. The line remained for some time afterwards and was lifted in 1983, the same year the signal box at Hayle was demolished. The line diverted away from the main line at the Hayle end of the viaduct and took a route down a short, sharp gradient. The ruling gradient was 1/27, and a catch point was present to stop any runaway wagons. This was purported to be the first catch point ever installed. The line then crossed a barrier level crossing on Hayle Terrace and passed over an iron swing bridge. This bridge carried both the railway and the road across to the quay. The line passed close beside Carnsew Pool before negotiating another level crossing, this time without gates or barriers. The train was now in the sidings area, called the quay. These sidings possessed no run around facility, therefore the trains for the wharves were propelled all the way from St Erth. The return journey saw the loco at the leading end of the movement.

The branch line to Hayle Wharves is a very important inclusion for the author. Growing up in Hayle Terrace, one knew a train was imminent because of the long tail backs of traffic. There was no bypass for the town in those days. This was the cue to run down the road to see the train carefully pass over the level crossing. The guard stood on the veranda of the leading guards van (as the train was being propelled). The barrier vehicles of old vent vans followed, then the four wheel oil tankers and finally the locomotive, often a Class 25. The author was fortunate to photograph three different classes of loco on the line: Class 08 which worked the final workings from 1981, Class 25 and Class 37. The Class 37 was a trial run that necessitated a St Blazey driver as Penzance crews did not sign the class. These only worked the train on a few occasions in 1980. The Class 25s worked the line from the end of the Warships in 1972 until traffic dwindled and a Class 08 was sufficient. The author was lucky to spend time as a child with George Willcocks who operated the ground frame at Hayle Wharves and shunted the train at the quay. He also visited the signal box at Hayle station when Percy Brookes was on duty, and found the principals of interlocking and the strict nature of railway operating procedures captivating. As the train ran on weekdays, it was only during the school holidays that the working of the branch could be enjoyed at close hand, and during term time, the wharves train was observed from Penpol school playground each lunchtime with friends.

The author was gifted some excellent photos (see pages) from the late John Lloyd of 25155 who drove the shunt tractor at the quay and these are included in his collection. The shunt tractor with road tyres positioned the tankers in the Esso depot.

The level crossing at Hayle Terrace is seen in this view of 08945 propelling the barrier wagons and brake van down to the wharves on a dull day in 1981. This was one of the final trains to visit. The train was only run to collect the discharged fuel tanks on this occasion. Note the unusual three-way barrier protection at this crossing, which was provided with five barriers. The crossing itself was wide despite there being only one track. This was a legacy of the former level crossing having multiple tracks branching out here to run to sidings to the left of the Sid Knowles lorry waiting at the single barrier from the wharves. Note that the Class 08 is fitted with a buck-eye-type coupling for the newly introduced HSTs at Long Rock. It was a very different trip on this day.

The black swing bridge near the level crossing is the frame for 25052, again propelling its train down to the wharf on a warm summer day in 1980. The guard can be seen keeping a lookout on the brake van veranda. There was a ground frame here (to the right of the locomotive), which allowed the bridge to swing, giving access to Carnsew pool. This bridge, which carried the railway and road, has since been replaced with a modern, fixed structure. The route from Hayle station to the wharves is now a footpath. The mineral wagons in the consist were barrier wagons provided between the brake van and oil tankers.

A superb over view of 25155 shunting at the quay taken by John Lloyd. The access to the Esso depot was via a scissors crossing, which is under the fuel tanks, close to the parked lorry. No loco visited there as it would be trapped with no run round! Therefore, a shunt tractor with road tyres was used to position the tankers in the depot. Shunting was often complex and fascinating to watch. Here, the Class 25 has both the full and discharged tanks coupled. The guards van and barrier wagons were cut off whilst the empty tanks were drawn forward, coupled to the full ones. The empties were then placed onto the brake van. The full tanks were then moved back into the sidings with the point leading to the fuel depot for the shunt tractor to push into position. The gates to the fuel depot have already been opened to the right. Just beyond this can be seen the entrance to the ICI depot, which was directly accessible by the train locomotive. All these manoeuvres were carried out with pedestrians, lorries and cars driving along the quay too! (Photo by John Lloyd)

Although the quality may be questionable, this image is one of the author's most treasured pictures. Few photographs exist of a Class 37 shunting at Hayle Wharves. The cars are as interesting as the train some might say! The author's father has cine film of 37299 visiting and this is 37206, one of the second allocation to visit the county in 1980, supplementing 37142 and 37267 at St Blazey in 1978. The Class 25s had vanished from Cornwall during 1980, so this was probably just after this period in the last months of the line being operational. Class 08s worked the final traffic, which had become rather sporadic in nature. One of the two chimneys from the former power station can be seen behind the train. These were blown up in 1983, and the local schools were excused from lessons to see this event. The author remembers a Class 50 on the up parcel train stopping on the viaduct to witness the spectacle. (Photo by John Lloyd)

In typical neglected condition, Plymouth Laira's 25052 stands on the quay shunting the oil tanks in the summer of 1980. The Class 25s were ideal for the Hayle Wharves branch as they were faster than a Class 08 along the main line run to and from St Erth and liked by the crews. The Class 25s replaced the Type 4 Warship class diesel hydraulics which had 2,200 horsepower compared to the 1,250 of the Type 2 Class 25. The black bridge by the level crossing was weight restricted, though tests were carried out with D1012 *Western Firebrand* in the 1970s to see if 100 tonne bogie tankers could be considered for use. The Western was allowed onto the bridge during a trial, which was successful, but none ever worked a train. The Class 37s, which weighed in at 105 tons, were the heaviest diesel locomotive to work a train down the branch.

Another shot from John Lloyd, this time of 25155 deeper back in the sidings at the quay. The domestic coal depot is more visible in this view, and a familiar Sid Knowles lorry is paying a visit. The St Ives branch and St Uny church are visible in the distance. The red oxide wagon loading shutes in the background point to wagons being loaded at Hayle Wharves.

25 052

Class	25-1
Weight tons	74
Brake force tons	38
RA	5
Max speed mph	90

LA

Penzance Driver Eddie Ralph pauses from shunting to give a smile to the camera at Hayle Wharves in 1980. Eddie is proudly wearing his recently received InterCity 125 badges on his lapels. However, his steed that day was anything but 125mph! This illustrates well the variety of trains driven by drivers years ago: express passenger, milk, parcels and freight, some in the same turn of duty.

Chapter 6

St Erth to St Ives

The St Ives line really is a jewel in the crown of Cornwall's railways. Countless excited holiday makers have looked out of the train window watching the coastline leisurely pass by on the five-mile trip. Until recently, most passenger journeys started from Lelant Saltings station. Opened in 1977, it was a pioneer of the park your car and catch the train to keep road traffic out of the congested, narrow roads in the resort. During the summer season of 1978, the author recalls six-car DMUs plodding back and forth, two coupled three-car Class 118 units. St Erth station is now the nominated park and ride station for the area to serve both Penzance and St Ives to minimise road traffic. The bay platform at St Erth has been widened to cater for the increased passenger loadings from there. The photos in this section are spread through the four seasons, and the beaches full of holiday makers in the summer months contrast nicely with the quieter months of the year.

Departing the bay platform at St Erth, the train passes the new car park and the former Milk Marketing Board buildings and heads towards the River Hayle. The largely unused station at Lelant Saltings is passed by and the line hugs the tidal river along the Hayle estuary. The small request stop of Lelant is next and the train leaves the estuary behind and climbs inland sharply towards St Uny church. As the train emerges from the cutting, the golden sands of Hayle Towans are visible, stretching as far as the eye can see towards Godrevy lighthouse. The train runs across the dunes on the opposing side of the River Hayle and the coastline opens out fully to reveal the Atlantic Ocean's splendour. The golf course is on the inland side of the train, but most passengers opt for the much more scenic coastal side of the train! Heading towards Carbis Bay, the railway line runs along a path along the cliff tops, the coast down below the train now. Carbis Bay station is next, and the train crosses the only masonry viaduct on the line and continues on its cliffside journey into St Ives. The line heads inland slightly and turns a final time towards the terminus at St Ives, with the yellow sand of Porthminster beach below laid out like a welcome mat beside the line.

A busy scene at St Erth sees one of the Class 122 single 'bubble' car units, set number P112, lead a Class 108 departing to St Ives in May 1992. 158714 can be seen in the bay siding, which was being tested for clearance along the line that day. Another mechanical DMU set is included in the picture, 871, a Class 108/101 hybrid set, sits in the up main platform with a Plymouth service.

From the 1960s, the Class 118 and 120 DMUs dominated the branch lines in Cornwall, supplemented by the single car 'Bubble' Class 121/122 units. This changed little through the 1970s until the late 1980s. The Class 117s originally based in the London area became familiar in the Duchy. These units were almost identical to the indigenous Class 118s. As the depots struggled to maintain the fleet, cascaded DMUs from other parts of the country became available, including Class 101s and 108s. The early 1990s saw the Network Southeast livery decorating the branch lines services. In 1993, a pair of two-car Class 117s led by set number L708 depart St Erth for St Ives, having nicely connected with a London-bound HST in the platform. As can be seen, only the bay siding remains, however the track bed left behind gives an idea of the once extensive sidings to the rear of the branch platform line.

The first stop along the line (until recently) was Lelant Saltings. This was the designated park and ride station from 1977 until 2019, which was used to stop cars cramming the narrow streets in St Ives itself. 150102 is seen departing for St Ives on 19 January 2017. The town of Hayle and St Elwyn's church are visible to the right of the train.

Looking quite incongruous in its Network Southeast livery, a Class 101 mechanical DMU approaches Lelant on a shuttle service between St Erth and St Ives on 19 March 1994. (Photo © Andy Thomas)

Approaching Lelant Saltings on the misty afternoon of 25 March 2007 is 37410 heading back to Penzance. This was the return of a trip aptly named the *St Ives Steamer* which ran as 1Z55, the 14:37 from Penzance to St Ives, with the Black 5 steam engine 45407. Just above the train, the white building of the former ICI building at Hayle Wharves can be seen. (Photo © Andy Thomas)

The line follows the Hayle estuary from Lelant Saltings station, an area of great interest to bird spotters. Many bird enthusiasts can be seen with their cameras and telescopes along the main causeway road between St Erth station and Hayle at all times of the year. On the odd occasion, they are outnumbered by loco enthusiasts, as on 14 June 2016. Up until 2018, St Erth signal box closed at night, so any test train workings were accommodated before the first branch service (just before 7am). This resulted in the Network Rail test train leaving St Erth for St Ives at around 05:30, bound for the resort. As it was mid-June, this resulted in a daylight run along the branch, just after sunrise. The train was headed by 37057 in original green livery and the train looked stunning running along the estuary as the sun rose, bathing the area in light. The train is passing the sleepy Lelant station heading for St Ives at a sedate pace.

A Class 50 visiting the branch on a Stumec crane-fitted Salmon wagon was an incredibly rare working. Route restrictions on the bridge next to Lelant Saltings had previously prohibited larger locomotives proceeding further than the sidings at St Erth. As the smaller locomotives disappeared from the network, exceptions were made. 50034 *Furious* is seen on a gloomy February Sunday afternoon parked up at Lelant station.

Railtours made a number of visits to St Ives once the weight restrictions on the bridge at Lelant Saltings were relaxed. On 19 March 1994, a trio of Class 50s worked *The Cornish Caper* charter to St Ives. 50033 *Glorious* was on the St Ives end, and 50007 *Sir Edward Elgar* and 50050 *Fearless* were on the St Erth end of the coaches. The outward bound train passes Lelant station.

As previously mentioned, keeping the increasingly ageing mechanical DMU fleet operating wasn't easy. The early 1990s saw the withdrawal of the newly introduced Class 155 sprinter units, which went into works to become single-car Class 153s. This resulted in older DMUs and loco-hauled stock being re-drafted into service. Branch loadings were growing, so at least three-car units were demanded in the summer on the St Ives branch. Some hybrid DMU formations cropped up, including this unusual three-car Class 117 set. Set number 117305 was at the time a two-car paring of the chocolate and cream DMBS trailer and Network Southeast DMS trailer. A fellow Class 117 DMBS trailer has been bolted on to form a three-car set. The colourful ensemble passes Lelant in the summer of 1991.

The sun was exceptionally golden on the late evening of 26 June 2011 and by the time this picture was taken it had also got really low in the sky forcing the driver of 150247 to pull down his screen visor as the unit headed for St Ives over the golf course at Lelant . (Photo © Andy Thomas)

Another view taken on 14 June 2016, this time of 37057 returning from St Ives and passing St Uny church. This image is taken from the Hayle power station beach car park at the mouth of the river. The author spent many hours on the beach here as a child enjoying the procession of DMUs working hard on jointed track climbing the stiff gradient from Lelant and yearned for a locomotive picture here. The bright morning sun is now much stronger for the return trip.

Winding the clock forward four years and the same train ran to St Ives at daybreak but just minutes prior to sunrise, regrettably. The train has gained an extra carriage in the formation, a former Caledonian Sleeper lounge car. This carriage has a toilet retention tank, which the yellow carriage loos do not have. Colas-liveried 37219 was provided at the Penzance end of the train on this occasion and is seen at Towan crossing on the golf course at Lelant just after 6am on 22 April 2020.

The view from the golf course at Lelant is breathtaking, if not a little hazardous due to the flying golf balls! The town of St Ives can be seen in the distance, and there is something to be said for the light there having a quality all of its own. The island is beautifully lit as a pair of Class 150 units, led by 150101, head for St Erth on 28 September 2015.

Another wonderful view, this time looking back at the Towans at Hayle as 150281 heads across the golf course at Lelant towards Carbis Bay and its destination of St Ives on 15 May 2010. (Photo © Andy Thomas)

This must surely be one of the most magnificent views from a train window in the whole of the country. A Wessex-liveried 150 heads over the golf course at Lelant, heading from St Erth to St Ives on 26 September 2006, giving passengers the glorious vista of St Ives bay, the golden sands at Hayle which stretch right along to Gwithian and, in the far distance, Godrevy lighthouse situated off Godrevy Point. (Photo © Andy Thomas)

It goes without saying that you can generally capture the daily mundane train in some sunshine but when something special comes along its another matter entirely. On a miserable day, when the sea mist had got a pronounced presence on the coast, D1015 *Western Champion* heads across the golf course at Lelant, heading for St Ives with the *East Lancs Champion* railtour on 16 May 2010. (Photo © Andy Thomas)

By the time the *East Lancs Champion* railtour left St Ives to return to Penzance, the mist that had been obstinate to clear, spoiling the view of the outward train, had lifted and it was brightening up. Making a bizarre but magnificent sight, 40145 makes its way back along the clifftops and through the tight curves at Carrack Gladden. Who would ever have thought that it would be possible to witness a Class 40 on the St Ives branch? (Photo © Andy Thomas)

On a glorious 26 June 2011, 150247 approaches Carbis Bay station with a St Erth to St Ives service. It is often said that artists have been drawn to the St Ives area over the years because the clear light makes colours look so bright and vivid and that certainly couldn't be denied on this particular day. (Photo © Andy Thomas)

50050 *Fearless* and 50007 *Sir Edward Elgar* work the *Cornish Caper* railtour back through Carbis Bay on a murky 19 March 1994.

Two Network Southeast-liveried two-car Class 101s, set numbers L839 and L842, depart Carbis Bay in the summer of 1993. The beach below is full of tourists, unlike the March picture taken previously.

The line follows the coast around to the small bridge at Hain Walk, which offers a wonderful view of St Ives. Class 150/1 150102 works the St Ives shuttle, a two-car unit sufficient for passenger loadings in early spring, on 17 March 2016.

The end of the line at the picturesque resort of St Ives. The station is well placed to serve the town and the two Class 150s were doing a good job shuttling people to and fro on 25 June 2011. Sadly though, judging by the amount of cars in the car park, the majority of people on the beach probably didn't arrive by train. (Photo © Andy Thomas)

An all-blue three-car Class 118, set number P480, waits custom at St Ives in the spring of 1980. The park and ride was not yet busy enough to warrant multiple sets. The passenger loadings saw two three-car units employed in the summers of 1978 and 1979.

Further reading from KEY
Publishing

As Europe's leading transport publisher, we produce a wide range of market-leading railway magazines.

Visit: shop.keypublishing.com for more details